Managing Editor
Karen J. Goldfluss, M.S. Ed.

Editor-in-Chief
Sharon Coan, M.S. Ed.

Illustrators
Howard Chaney
Bruce Hedges

Cover Artist
Lesley Palmer

Art Coordinator
Kevin Barnes

Art Director
CJae Froshay

Imaging
Rosa C. See

Product Manager
Phil Garcia

Publisher
Mary D. Smith, M.S. Ed.

Matter

SUPER SCIENCE ACTIVITIES

Written by Ruth M. Young, M.S. Ed.

Teacher Created Resources, Inc.
6421 Industy Way
Westminster, CA 92683
wwwteachercreated.com

©2002 Teacher Created Resources, Inc.
Reprinted, 2005

Made in the U. S. A.
ISBN-0-7439-3660-4

Table of Contents

Introduction

Everything is made of matter, and all matter occupies space. The amount of matter in an object is called *mass*. Earth's gravity gives the mass of the object *weight*. If that object were go to into space, where there is no gravity, it would lose its <u>weight</u> but not its <u>mass</u>.

The physical properties of certain kinds of matter can be recognized through the sense of touch, sight, smell, taste, or hearing. Matter usually exists in three states – solid, liquid, and gas. There are four more, <u>rare</u> stages of matter which only exist in extreme high or low temperatures. They are: *plasmas, superfluids, superconductors, and Bose-Einstein condensates.*

Matter can undergo physical change by changing the temperature. For example, water turns to ice when frozen, this ice melts into water when it gets warm, and then evaporates into vapor (gas) when heated even more.

Matter is made up of chemical elements. It can change chemically, as in the case of cooking when various matter is combined to produce a cake.

The solid objects we use everyday are made up of molecules and crystals. These structures consist of atoms that are linked together. An atom is made up of particles called *protons*, *neutrons,* and *electrons*. Protons and neutrons, which make up most of the atom's mass, are composed of pointlike units known as *quarks*. Scientists have not yet determined if quarks can be broken down into smaller bits. Electrons are also considered to be pointlike. Particles smaller than an atom are called *subatomic particles*.

Differences in electric charges hold the atom together. Protons have a positive charge, and neutrons are electrically neutral, so the nucleus as a whole is positively charged. Electrons are negatively charged. Because opposite charges attract, an electric force tends to keep the electrons in place.

Electrons whirl around the nucleus in layers called *electron shells*. The electrons in the outermost shells are not tightly bound to the nucleus. As a result, some outer electrons can be shared by two atoms in a *chemical bond*, a linking of atoms. The atoms in molecules are bound in this way. Outer electrons can also jump from one atom to another, producing positive and negative <u>ions</u> (charged atoms). Ions can bond to form crystals, such as table salt, which is a crystal consisting of positive sodium ions and negative chloride ions.

The activities in this book allow students to investigate matter through their senses and simple experiments. They learn about the properties of matter and the physical and chemical changes.

What's Cooking?

Overview: *Students investigate the physical properties of popcorn.*

Materials

- popcorn maker
- Fun with Popcorn Level A and B data sheets (pages 5 and 6)

Lesson Preparation

- Begin to make popcorn so it will be well underway as the students enter the classroom.

Activity

1. As students enter the classroom they should smell but not see the popcorn being made. Have them get seated and then use the following questions to discuss the popcorn with them.
   - How do you know popcorn is being made? (*the smell and popping sound*)
   - What do you use to smell the popcorn? (*nose*)
   - How is the smell of popcorn reaching your nose? (*through the air*)
   - What do you use to hear the popcorn popping? (*ears*)
   - How is the sound of the popping reaching your ears? (*also through the air*)
2. Show them the popcorn and then ask how they can be sure it is popcorn. (*They can see it.*)
3. Ask them what they use to see the popcorn. (*eyes*)
4. List the senses on the board beside the part of the body used for that sense.
5. Have the students tell you what other senses they could use to be sure this is popcorn (*taste and feel or touch*). Add these to the list of senses and parts of the body.
6. Distribute popcorn, asking each student to take one piece, feel it, and then describe how it feels to a partner.
7. Have students chew the popcorn slowly before swallowing. Let them describe the taste to a partner.

Closure

- Distribute Level A or Level B data sheet to each student according to ability. Let the students complete the data sheet to summarize the use of their senses which helped them investigate the properties of popcorn.

What's Cooking?

Fun with Popcorn—Level A

Name:_____ Date: _____

To the Student: You have just had a chance to learn about popcorn by using your senses. Fill in the missing words and make drawings to help you review what senses you used for each thing you did with the popcorn. One letter of each missing word is given to you to give you a hint.

1. When you first came into the room, you could ___ ___ E ___ ___ popcorn being made.

   Draw the part of your body you used for this.

2. You could also tell it was popcorn because you could ___ ___ ___ R it popping.

   Draw the part of your body you used for this.

3. The teacher showed you the popcorn so you could S ___ ___ the popcorn.

   Draw the part of the body you used for this.

4. The teacher gave you some popcorn and told you to ___ ___ ___ L it.

   Draw the part of the body you used for this.

5. Finally, the teacher let you ___ ___ S ___ ___ the popcorn.

   Draw the part of the body you used for this.

5

What's Cooking? *(cont.)*

Fun with Popcorn—Level B

Name:_____ Date: _____

To the Student: You have just had a chance to learn about popcorn by using your senses. Fill in the missing words and make drawings to help you review what senses you used for each thing you did with the popcorn. Write what each sense told you about the popcorn.

1. When you first came into the room, you could_____popcorn being made.

   Draw the part of your body you used for this.
   Tell what this sense told you about the popcorn.

2. You could also tell it was popcorn because you could_____it making noise.

   Draw the part of your body you used for this.
   Tell what this sense told you about the popcorn.

3. The teacher showed you the popcorn so you could_____the popcorn.

   Draw the part of the body you used for this.
   Tell what this sense told you about the popcorn.

4. The teacher gave you some popcorn and told you to_____it.

   Draw the part of the body you used for this.
   Tell what this sense told you about the popcorn.

5. Finally, the teacher let you_____the popcorn.

   Draw the part of the body you used for this.
   Tell what this sense told you about the popcorn.

Identifying Matter by Sound and Feel

> ## Teacher Information
> ### *Investigating Physical Properties of Matter*
>
> This series of activities should be spread over several days. Some can be done in learning centers, while others are for the class to do together. The activities are designed to have students develop the use of their senses while investigating the physical properties of various types of matter. These will include using the senses of smell, taste, sound, touch, and sight.

Overview: *Students will investigate the physical properties of sound that matter can make.*

Materials

- opaque, empty film canister for each student, available free at most places where film is developed
- trays (one per group)
- parent letter (page 9)
- Sound and Feel Containers List (page 10)
- What's Inside the Container? Data Sheet (page 11)
- transparency of the Sound and Feel Containers List (page 10) and Sound and Feel Answers (page 12)

Lesson Preparation

- Send home the parent letter and a film canister for each student a few days in advance of when you conduct the activities.
- Put a number on each container, both on the lid and on the canister as they are returned. Record each student's name and container number on the Sound and Feel Containers List.
- Select 10 canisters to use and save the rest for later. Make a random list of their contents as an answer sheet.
- Students will then match the characteristics they sense when shaking the containers and copy the name of the item from the answer list beside the container's number.

Identifying Matter by Sound and Feel *(cont.)*

Activity

1. Divide the students into small groups and then distribute a copy of the What's Inside the Container? Data Sheet to each group. Divide the containers into sets for each group and distribute them on a tray.

2. Have the students carefully shake the containers to see if they can guess the contents. The members of the group should come to agreement and then record their guess.

3. Rotate the containers on the trays to another group until all containers have been tested by each group. It is important to allow enough time for each group to discuss the possibilities before recording their guess.

4. Monitor the students to be sure the lids are not removed. Be certain that each member of the group is contributing to the test and discussion.

Closure

- Have each group tell what they thought was in each container. Record their guesses on the Sound and Feel Guess List transparency.

- Show the containers transparency (page 10) of the list of items in the containers along with the items themselves.

- Have the students check to see how many they could guess correctly just by hearing the sound and feeling the contents move.

- Discuss what helped them guess these items correctly.

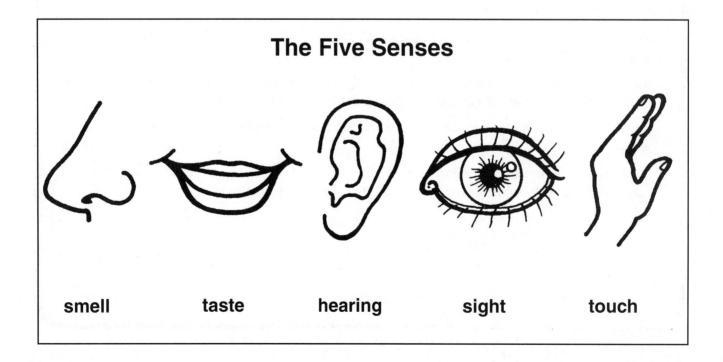

The Five Senses

smell   taste   hearing   sight   touch

Date_____

Dear Parents,

We are learning about the properties of matter and will be doing an activity that uses the senses of hearing and touch to identify various types of matter. Each student has been given a film canister to put some type of matter inside. Please help them find something that is appropriate to place inside the canister. Put something which makes a sound when shaken inside the canister. Be sure there is only one type of matter in each container. The canister should not be filled so full that the contents cannot make a sound when shaken gently.

What do I hear?

Suggestions for matter which might be included in the container:

- sand
- pebble(s)
- water
- paper clip(s)

- rubber eraser
- coin(s)
- marble(s)
- cork

Students are encouraged to put something unusual in their containers.

Thank you for helping to make our activity exciting. You are welcome to join our class when we do this activity on_____.

Sincerely,

_____

Identifying Matter by Sound and Feel *(cont.)*

Sound and Feel Containers List

Student Names	Contents
1.	
2.	
3.	
4.	
5.	
6.	
7.	
8.	
9.	
10.	
11.	
12.	
13.	
14.	
15.	
16.	
17.	
18.	
19.	
20.	
21.	
22.	
23.	
24.	
25.	
26.	
27.	
28.	
29.	
30.	

Identifying Matter by Sound and Feel *(cont.)*

What's Inside the Container? Data Sheet

Name:_____ Date: _____

To the Student: DO NOT OPEN THE LID. Shake the container and listen to the sound it makes.
How does it feel when you shake it? Can you guess what is inside? Look at the answer list. Choose
the name of the thing you think is inside the container and write it next to the container's number.

1.	
2.	
3.	
4.	
5.	
6.	
7.	
8.	
9.	
10.	

Identifying Matter by Sound and Feel *(cont.)*

Sound and Feel Answers

To the Teacher: List the items in the canisters in random order below. This will be the answer list for students to use.

1.	
2.	
3.	
4.	
5.	
6.	
7.	
8.	
9.	
10.	

Identifying Matter by Smell

Overview: *Students will investigate the physical properties of smell of matter.*

Materials

- opaque empty film canister for each student
- masking tape
- parent letter (page 14)
- Smell Containers List (page 15)
- copies and a transparency of What's Inside the Container? Data Sheet (page 16)

Lesson Preparation

- Send home the parent letter and a film canister for each student a few days in advance of conducting the activities.
- Put a number on each container, both on the lid and the canister as they are returned. Record each student's name and container number on the Smell Containers List.
- Before doing the smell activity, put a hole about the diameter of a pencil in the middle of each lid with a drill or awl. Cover the hole with masking tape until the activity is to begin.
- Use only 10 containers at one time to make it easier for students to identify them.
- This lesson may be simplified by listing the contents of the containers in random order on the board. Students will then match the characteristics they sense when smelling the containers and put the container number next to the item on the list which they think is inside.

Activity

1. Divide the students into small groups and then distribute a copy of the data sheet What's Inside the Container? to each group. Divide the containers among the groups.
2. Have the students carefully lift the tape and smell the contents of each container and then record the guess agreed upon by the group on the record sheet. They should seal the tape over the hole again.
3. Rotate the containers on the trays to another group until all containers have been tested by each group. It is important to allow enough time for each group to discuss the possibilities before recording their guess.
4. Monitor the students to be sure the lids are not removed. Be certain that each member of the group is contributing to the test and discussion.

Closure

- Have groups tell what they thought was in each container. Record their number guesses on the board beside the list of items.
- Give them the correct answers.
- Have students see how many they could guess correctly just by the smell of the contents.
- Discuss what helped them guess these items correctly.

Parent Letter for Smell Containers

Date_____

Dear Parents,

We are learning about the properties of matter and will be doing an activity that uses the sense of smell to identify various types of matter. Each student has been given a film canister to put some type of matter inside. Please help your child find something that is appropriate to place inside the canister. Put something in the container which will give off a smell. Be sure there is only one type of matter in each container.

What do I smell?

When the canister is returned to school, a hole the size of a pencil diameter will be drilled in the lid. If the matter is liquid (e.g., vinegar), please use a cotton ball or piece of paper and put a few drops of the liquid on it. This will prevent the liquid from spilling out the hole in the lid. A piece of tape will be put over the hole to prevent evaporation.

Suggestions for matter which might be included in the container follow:

- slice of apple
- piece of banana
- water
- vanilla flavoring

- shampoo
- peppermint flavoring
- perfume
- slice of onion

Students are encouraged to put something unusual in their containers.

Thank you for helping make our activity exciting. You are welcome to join our class when we do this activity on_____.

Sincerely,

_____

Identifying Matter by Smell *(cont.)*

Smell Containers List

Student Names	Contents
1.	
2.	
3.	
4.	
5.	
6.	
7.	
8.	
9.	
10.	
11.	
12.	
13.	
14.	
15.	
16.	
17.	
18.	
19.	
20.	
21.	
22.	
23.	
24.	
25.	
26.	
27.	
28.	
29.	
30.	

Identifying Matter by Smell *(cont.)*

What's Inside the Container? Data Sheet

Name:_____ Date: _____

To the Student: DO NOT REMOVE the lid of your container. Lift the tape on the lid and sniff through the small hole. Can you guess what is making the smell? Find the number of the container on the list and write your guess of what is making the smell beside that number.

1.	
2.	
3.	
4.	
5.	
6.	
7.	
8.	
9.	
10.	

Identifying Matter by Taste

Overview: *Students will investigate the taste of various types of matter to be identified.*

Materials

- cotton-tipped swabs
- paper plates
- 6–8 flavorful solid and liquid foods
- copy of Taste Guess List (page 18) for each student

- 1-ounce (30 mL) cups
- toothpicks
- blindfold or sleep mask

Lesson Preparation

- Select a variety of flavors for students to taste and identify—e.g., salt crystals, sugar crystals, vinegar, and small pieces of fruit. Avoid flavors which might be disliked, such as onions.
- Place these in cups or on paper plates appropriate to the food. Pieces to be tasted should be about the size of a quarter.
- List the items being tested to make an answer key.
- Have other adults or older students assist in this activity since the taste test is given individually.
- Set up the testing site where no other student can observe. More than one site may be arranged if there are enough assistants and room so the answers will not be overheard.
- Set up a rotation for students to come to the site(s).
- The lesson may be simplified by providing a list of flavors to match as students taste the samples. To make it more challenging, add to the list flavors which will not be tested.

(**Caution:** Check to see whether any students are not permitted to eat any of the foods you are using.)

Activity

1. Explain that you are going to test students' sense of taste, seeing how many things they can identify by taste alone. Tell them they will be tested individually and should not tell anyone else what they tasted. You want them to keep this secret until all have been tested.
2. Put the name of the student being tested on a copy of the Taste Guess List. Blindfold the student who is to be tested.
3. Dip a cotton swab into the liquid and let the student place it on the tip on the tongue to test its flavor and guess what it is. Use a different swab for each flavor.
4. Pick up solid foods with a toothpick and let the child place it in his or her mouth to chew.
5. Always give the items to be tasted in the same order and permit time for students to think about the flavor before guessing. After each flavor is tasted, record the guess on the list.

Closure

- When all students have been tested, share the results of their guesses. Give them the correct tastes for each of the tests.
- Ask students what clues they used to identify flavors.
- Suggest that they try eating an evening meal with a blindfold to see how many foods they can identify by flavor and texture.

Identifying Matter by Taste (cont.)

Taste Guess List

Name: _____

1.
2.
3.
4.
5.
6.
7.
8.

Identifying Matter by Touch

Overview: *Students will investigate matter through the sense of touch.*

Materials

- small coffee can
- wide packing tape
- This Is My Guess form (page 20)
- large sock with elastic ribbing
- variety of items to place in the can
- children's story which relates to this activity

Lesson Preparation

- Cut the cuff off the sock. Slip the cuff over the coffee can and tape the cut edge to the can. The cuff should be about the length of the can. The contents in the can cannot be seen, but the hand can reach in to feel it. Tape the other end of the cloth to the can.
- Collect items for the can with a variety of properties (texture, density, shape, and hardness). Items might include such things as fruit, a glove, a marble, or scissors. Use items which students have had experience with so they can identify them by memory.
- Make a box for students to place their guesses in to identify the daily mystery object.

Activity

1. Tell students they are going to see how much they can tell about an object just by feeling it. Tell them you have put something inside a coffee can and you want them to stick a hand inside (demonstrate this) to feel the object. They should feel it to tell its shape, size, weight, and texture. When they are finished feeling it, they should pass the can to the next person. It is very important that students keep their ideas secret. Let them understand that they will first be asked to describe the object and then tell what they think it is.
2. Tell the students that you will read a story to them as they feel what is in the can. Send the can around the classroom so each student may feel the object inside as you read the story aloud. Monitor them to be sure no one gives clues to anyone else.
3. When the story ends and all have felt the object, have students work in small groups and describe the item as if they were telling someone who had not had the chance to feel it.
4. Now tell the groups to come to an agreement of what they thought was inside the can. Show several items and let the students see which fits their descriptions.
5. Explain that a new item will be placed in the can each day and students will guess what they think is inside based on how it feels. Show the forms which they will use for writing their guesses and the box in which they can place them each day.

Closure

- At the end of each day, read the guesses and show the object.
- Encourage students to bring something of their own to place inside the can.

Identifying Matter by Touch *(cont.)*

To the Teacher: Two copies of this form are provided to help you save paper.

This Is My Guess

Name:_____ Date:_____

Draw a picture to show what the thing inside the can might look like.

I think a_____is inside the can.

This Is My Guess

Name:_____ Date:_____

Draw a picture to show what the thing inside the can might look like.

I think a_____is inside the can.

From Solid to Liquid

Overview: *Students observe ice changing from a solid to a liquid.*

Materials

- 1-ounce (30 mL) cups (one per student)
- ice cubes (one per student)
- The Story of My Ice Cube Data Sheet (page 22)

Lesson Preparation

- Place the small cups on a tray and fill them with water.
- Place them in a freezer to form an ice cube for each student.

Activity

1. Ask the students if they have ever played with ice. Let them share their experiences.
2. Divide the students into small groups and tell them that you are going to give everyone an ice cube. Explain that you want them to play with it and tell their group members what they find out about the ice as they watch it melt.
3. Give each student an ice cube on a dish. Encourage the students to find out everything they can about their ice cubes. Permit them to touch and hold their ice cubes as well as breathe on them.

Closure

- Distribute a copy of the data sheet The Story of My Ice Cube for students to complete.
- Have the students share their ice cube stories with the members of their group.
- Save the cups of water for the next lesson in this series.

From Solid to Liquid *(cont.)*

The Story of My Ice Cube Data Sheet

Name: _____ Date: _____

Draw four pictures to show what happened to your ice cube as you watched it melt.

1	**2**
3	**4**

Write about what you saw happen to your ice cube as it melted.

From Liquid to Gas

Overview: *Students will observe water change into vapor (gas).*

Materials

- hot plate
- dark food coloring
- cups of water used in previous lesson
- heat-proof clear glass container
- large cooking thermometer used in making candy
- permanent black marker
- What Happened to the Water? Data Sheet (page 25)

Lesson Preparation

- Mark the glass container off in $^1/_2$ inch (1 cm) intervals with the permanent marker.
- Arrange the classroom so the students will be able to observe this demonstration. Place the hot plate on the table and arrange seating for the students around the table at a safe distance.
- Set the hot plate on its lowest setting and turn it on to preheat it.

From Liquid to Gas *(cont.)*

Activity

1. Review what the students observed as they watched their ice cubes melt in the previous activity. Ask them to tell you why their ice melted. (*The ice melted because it was too warm.*) Ask them what they think will happen if you pour the water from their melted ice cubes into the glass container and then set it on the hot plate.

2. Give each student a cup of water and let him or her pour it into the glass container. Add a drop of dark food coloring to make the water visible. Have the students notice where the water level is on the container. Use the marker and place the #1 next to the marker at the top of the water level. Number the other marks to the bottom of the container beginning with #2, etc.

3. Put the thermometer into the water and have the students look at the level of the liquid in the thermometer. Write the temperature on the board. Continue to write the temperature on the board as the water heats up and begins to boil.

4. Place the container on the hot plate and turn up the heat. Have the students observe what is happening. Leave the thermometer in the water. As they observe, ask them questions such as those below.

   • What do you see in the water? (*Bubbles will begin to form as it gets hotter.*)

   • Is the water getting warmer? How do you know? (*The thermometer liquid is rising.*)

   • Do you see anything in the container other than water? (*Steam will begin to appear.*)

5. As the water begins to boil, point out that the bubbles are bigger and that the water is in motion. Show the steam rising from the water. Have students note the water level. Ask them where they think the steam is coming from and where it is going. (*The steam is coming from the water, and it is going into the air.*)

6. Continue to record the temperature of the water (*it should level off once it begins to boil*), and point out the level of the water as it drops. Stop the demonstration before the container boils dry. Remove the container from the hot plate and place it on a pot holder on the table.

Closure

• Ask the students what they think will happen to the rest of the water in the container. (*It will evaporate, turn to gas, and become part of the atmosphere.*)

• Discuss what they observed, being sure they understand that the water turned to gas when it was heated.

• Distribute the What Happened to the Water? Data Sheet for students to complete. Permit them to discuss this with other students as they work on the data sheet.

From Liquid to Gas *(cont.)*

What Happened to the Water? Data Sheet

Name:_____ Date: _____

Draw four pictures to show what happened to the water as you watched it being heated.

1	2

3	4

Write about what you saw happen to the water as it was heated.

From Gas to Liquid

Overview: *Students will observe two different methods for turning gas to liquid.*

Materials

- tall, clear glass
- blue food coloring
- blue ice cubes
- hot plate
- heat-proof glass container
- aluminum pie pan
- ring stand or other support to hold pie pan
- 3-inch (7.5 cm) square of dark construction paper

Lesson Preparation

- Make blue ice cubes by adding coloring to the water to make it dark blue and then freeze it.
- Add a few drops of coloring to the heat-proof glass container and fill it half full of water. Place it on the hot plate. Put the ring stand next to the hot plate and then put the pie pan on the ring stand so that it is about 3 inches (7.5 cm) above the container.

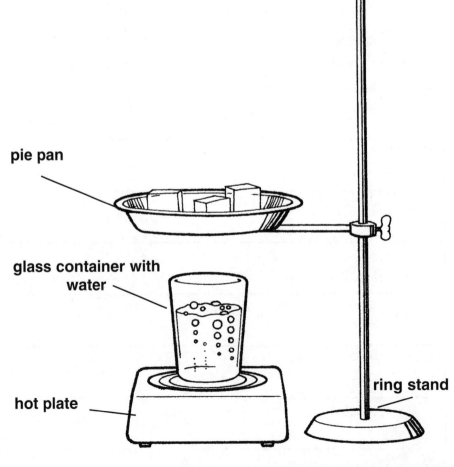

pie pan

glass container with water

hot plate

ring stand

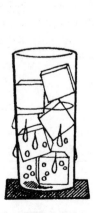

From Gas to Liquid *(cont.)*

Activity

1. Seat the students near the table. Explain that you are going to heat the water with the hot plate. Ask them what will happen when the water is heated. They should remember this from the last lesson.

2. As the water is heating, begin the other demonstration. Put a few drops of coloring in the tall glass and then fill it half full of water. Add 5–6 blue ice cubes. Have one of the students feel the outside of the glass and tell if it is wet or dry. Show the students the colored paper so they may see that it is also dry. Place the paper under the glass. The glass should be at least 3 feet (90 cm) away from the hot plate.

3. Place some blue ice cubes in the pie pan. Have the students discuss what they think will happen to the ice as the container of water below it is heated.

4. As the water begins to boil, ask questions which will help students look for details as they observe the changes. Some examples are provided below. If students do not know the answers, give them the answers so they will be able to follow the process.

   • Where is the steam coming from? (*It comes from the boiling water.*)

   • Why is the water turning to steam? (*The water is being heated and is evaporating.*)

   • What color is the steam? (*It is white or clear.*)

   • Why isn't it blue like the water? (*When water turns to gas [evaporates] anything added to that water, such as the coloring, is left behind.*)

   • What color is the water which is forming on the bottom of the pie pan. (*It is clear.*)

   • Do you think this water is leaking from the pie pan? (*No, because it is clear, not blue.*)

   • Where did it come from? (*It came from the steam hitting the cold bottom of the pan where it then condensed into a liquid again.*)

Closure

   • Show the glass of blue ice water which has been sitting on the table. Have students observe that the construction paper is wet, and so is the outside of the glass. Wipe the condensation off the glass with a white tissue to show that it is not blue.

   • Ask the students where this water came from. They may think it has leaked out of the glass, but tell them to look at the color of the water inside and that on the tissue so they will realize that it has not leaked. Explain that just like the steam hitting the cold pie pan, there is water vapor (gas) in the air. When the air hits a cold surface, the water vapor changes to liquid water.

Dance of the Molecules

Teacher Information

The *molecule* is one of the basic units of matter. It is the smallest particle into which a substance can be divided and still have the chemical properties of the original substance. If the substance were divided further, only atoms of the chemical elements would remain. For example, a drop of water contains billions of water molecules. If the drop could be divided into a single water molecule, it would still have all the chemical properties of water. But if the water molecule were divided, only atoms of the elements hydrogen and oxygen would remain.

Molecules are always in motion. Molecules in a solid, such as water ice, are packed closely and move very little, vibrating around a point where they balance between the other molecules. Molecules in liquid water are moving slowly but cling together loosely. Molecules in gaseous matter, such as steam, are moving so fast that they can separate and become light enough to mingle with molecules in the atmosphere.

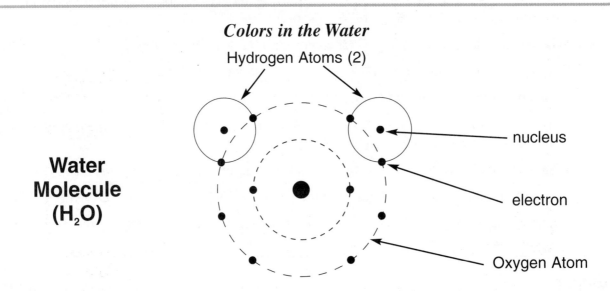

Colors in the Water

Hydrogen Atoms (2)

nucleus

electron

Water Molecule (H₂O)

Oxygen Atom

Overview: *Students will learn about the motions of water molecules in solid, liquid, and gaseous states.*

To the Teacher: This lesson is divided into two sections—a teacher demonstration and a student activity which has the students conduct the experiment demonstrated by the teacher. It is best to do these on two separate days to allow sufficient time for each of them.

Teacher Demonstration

Materials

- 3 large clear containers, at least 2-quart (2 liter) capacity
- dropper bottle of blue, red, or green food coloring
- hot, warm, and ice water
- Student Activity Data Sheet (page 30)
- crayons to match the color used in the demonstration

Dance of the Molecules *(cont.)*

Colors in the Water *(cont.)*

Teacher Demonstration *(cont.)*

1. Prepare file cards with the labels *Hot*, *Cold*, and *Warm* to place near the containers.

2. Fill one of the large containers with tap water and let it sit long enough to reach room temperature. This will be the warm water needed for the demonstration. Place the three containers where they can be seen by all the students. Just before beginning the demonstration, fill the second container with very hot water and the third with ice water.

3. Tell the students that you are going to do a demonstration and that you want them to watch very carefully to see what happens. Explain that they should be ready to tell you what they saw after the demonstration is over.

4. Carefully put one drop of food coloring into each container. A beautiful display is created as the coloring spreads in different ways in the three jars. The coloring in the hot water will quickly disperse; in the warm water it will spread more slowly; in the cold water it will spread across the surface and then gradually sink and begin to mix with the water.

   (The coloring will look somewhat like the drawings below within a minute of the drops entering the water.)

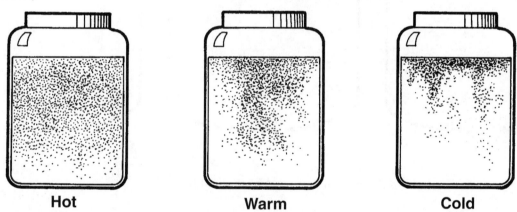

| Hot | Warm | Cold |

5. Discuss what the students have seen thus far, urging them to share as many details as possible. Tell them to compare the difference in the way the coloring spread in the different temperatures of water.

Closure

- As the students continue doing other activities, stop periodically to have them look at the changes in the water. Note these on the board. Be sure they know that nothing is stirring the water, yet the coloring continues to spread.

- After the coloring has spread through the hot water but is still not completely mixed in the other containers, distribute the data sheet (page 30) and have the students make drawings to show what the water looks like. Be sure the students are drawing the correct image for each temperature.

- Have the students share their drawings and ideas of what is happening.

   (Do not give any answers at this time. This demonstration is designed to give the students an opportunity to guess what is happening based only on their observations.)

Colors in the Water—Student Activity Data Sheet

Name:_____ Date: _____

Use a crayon to show what the coloring looks like in the water.

Hot	**Warm**	**Cold**

Write what you think is making the coloring spread in the water.

_____

_____

_____

_____

_____

_____

_____

_____

_____

Dance of the Molecules *(cont.)*

Colors in the Water—Student Activity Lesson

Materials (for eight groups of students)

- 24 clear plastic 9-ounce (270 mL) cups
- hot, warm, and ice water
- 8 small dropper bottles of food coloring (red, blue, and green)
- overhead projector
- toothpick
- 8 trays
- green, red, and blue crayons
- Colors in the Water Data Sheet (page 33)

Lesson Preparation

- Use a permanent marker to write *Hot* on a third of the cups, *Cold* on another third, and *Warm* on the last. Mark the large jars in the same manner.
- Fill a large container with water and let it reach room temperature; this will be the warm water for the activity.
- Heat water on a hot plate. This water will be mixed with tap water in the jar and cups so that it is hotter than the warm water.
- Just before doing the activity, fill the cold and warm cups with water, placing ice in the cold cups. Fill the hot cups nearly full of tap water and add the hot water. (*Caution:* Students will be testing the water temperature with their fingers, so be sure the hot water will not burn them.)
- Prepare a tray for each group with the three cups of water, dropper bottle of food coloring, and enough crayons (which match the food coloring) for each child in the group.

Activity *(Note: If this activity is too difficult for the students, do only the teacher demonstration to explain the motion of molecules.)*

1. Turn on the overhead projector and put a drop of clear water on the glass. Explain that you are going to try to make this drop of water as tiny as possible by pulling it apart with a toothpick. Using the toothpick, separate the water into the smallest drop possible.

2. Explain that even though this water drop is too small to be divided any further, it contains billions of tiny parts called *molecules*, so small they cannot even be seen clearly with the most powerful microscope. Tell students that all matter is made of molecules, even the air we breathe, the water we drink, and our own bodies. Explain the motion of molecules in the various states of matter; solid, liquid, and gas. (See Teacher Information, page 28.) Tell the students that although molecules cannot be seen, their motion can be.

3. Remind the students of the demonstration you did which used large containers of water and coloring to show the molecules in motion. Tell the students that it is now their turn to experiment with the motion of water molecules.

Dance of the Molecules *(cont.)*

Colors in the Water—Student Activity Lesson *(cont.)*

Activity *(cont.)*

4. Add hot water to the cups marked *Hot*. Divide the students into small groups and distribute a tray of materials to each group. Let the students feel the water so they can see that it is cold, warm, and hot. Tell them that they are going to put a drop of food coloring into each cup of water and then watch to see what happens to the coloring. Caution them not to shake or stir the water so that they can observe the motion of the molecules.

5. Distribute the Dance of the Molecules data sheet and review it with the students. Tell them to put a crayon on their paper so they will be ready to begin making a drawing of what they see happening as soon as the drops are placed in three cups. Have them wait for you to signal when to drop the coloring into the water.

6. After all containers have coloring in them, tell the students to draw what the water looked like when the drops first entered the water.

7. About 7–10 minutes after the drops were added, have the students make another drawing of their three cups.

8. Explain that the drops of coloring plunge into the water because of the force behind them, just like a diver going into the water. The drop of coloring is also pulled down by gravity. Tell the students to look again at their cups of water and discuss any changes they see.

Closure

- Tell the students they are now going to do the Dance of the Molecules. Move the class to the playground or cafeteria.

    a. Gather the students together in a tight group to simulate molecules of water in a solid (ice). They should be squeezed tightly together and only able to jiggle slightly in place.

    b. Have them move further apart, holding hands to simulate molecules of water in a liquid.

    c. Finally, tell them to release hands and move far apart to simulate molecules of water in a vapor.

- Return to the classroom and have the students observe their cups of water. (*The coloring should be completely mixed in most of them by now.*) Look at the large jars and have the students explain what they see. Be sure they know that the molecules of hot water move faster than those in cold water. This is demonstrated by the coloring mixing faster in the hot water.

- Ask the students to answer the questions on their data sheet and then discuss them.

Dance of the Molecules *(cont.)*

Colors in the Water—Data Sheet

Name:_____ Date: _____

Use the crayon to show what the food coloring did when it first was dropped into the cups of water.

Hot   **Warm**   **Cold**

Use the crayon to show what the water looks like now that the food coloring has been in it for_____minutes.

Hot   **Warm**   **Cold**

What made the coloring mix with the water? _____

_____

Why did the coloring spread at different rates in each of the cups? _____

_____

_____

Liquid + Solid = Gas

Teacher Information

Investigating Chemical Changes of Matter

Changes in the chemical composition of matter are called *chemical changes*. An example of this is when vinegar and baking soda are combined. The result is carbon dioxide gas. Another chemical change occurs when iron combines with oxygen in moist air to form iron oxide. This process is called *oxidation* and the result is the formation of rust.

The following activities are designed for young children to do and will enable them to observe safe chemical changes of matter.

Overview: *Students will create a chemical change by combining vinegar and baking soda. (**Caution:** To avoid students getting the mixture in their eyes, have them wear safety goggles and use only the small quantities of vinegar and baking soda suggested in this lesson.)*

Materials

- vinegar, baking soda, salt, sugar, flour
- trays
- small Styrofoam plates and plastic spoons
- 3 oz. (90 mL) paper cups
- Which One Fizzes? Data Sheet (page 36)
- dropper bottles or micropipets (can be ordered from Carolina Biological—Resources section)

Lesson Preparation

- Fill micropipets or dropper bottles with vinegar.
- Divide the cups into sets of four and mark them *Flour*, *Baking Soda*, *Sugar*, and *Salt*.
- Put about a teaspoon of each powder (e.g., flour) into the cups labeled with its name.
- Divide the plate into quarters with a marking pen and label the quarters with the powders' names.
- For each group of students prepare trays which will have a pipet of vinegar, set of four cups of the powders, plate, spoon, and paper towel.

Liquid + Solid = Gas *(cont.)*

Activity

Note: *If this lesson is too difficult for the level of the students, it may be done as a demonstration in small groups with the students recording their observations.*

1. Explain to students that they are going to do an experiment using four solids and one liquid. Tell them what these solids and liquid are. Caution them that when scientists do experiments they are very careful when mixing things. Also tell them that scientists watch closely to see what happens when things are mixed together.

2. Divide students into small groups, distribute the tray of materials, and familiarize the students with each item on the tray. (Have students practice first with water-filled pipets to learn to control the amount of drops.)

3. Give each student a copy of the data sheet and review it with them. Tell them that they are to rotate the responsibility of putting drops of vinegar on the white powders. Explain that you will tell them which powders to test. Have students use the spoon to place a very small amount of white powder in each quarter as you call out the powder, doing baking soda last.

4. Tell students to put a few drops of vinegar on the flour and then record what happens on their data sheet. Continue through the powders, saving baking soda for last.

Closure

- Have students share the results from their data sheets.

Extender Demonstration

To the Teacher: If appropriate for the students' level of understanding, demonstrate that the gas given off by the combination of vinegar and baking soda is carbon dioxide.

- You will need vinegar, baking soda, a wide-mouthed jar, a small clear cup, and three long matches.

- Place several teaspoons of baking soda into the jar. Light a match and hold it in the jar above the baking soda. (*The flame continues to burn.*)

- Pour a tablespoon of vinegar into a small clear cup. Light a match and hold it in the cup above the vinegar. (*The flame continues to burn.*)

- Pour the vinegar over the baking soda. (*The bubbles and froth which result are a chemical change.*) When the gas bubbles appear, light another match and place it near the bubbles. (*The flame will be extinguished.*)

- Ask the students to tell what they observed, providing as much detail as they can. Tell them to think of reasons why the match went out.

- After they have the chance to discuss what they saw, explain that when the vinegar and baking soda mixed, they created a chemical change in both of them, which became a gas. This gas is carbon dioxide, which is heavier than the gas in the air, and it smothered the flame. Tell them that the flame continued to burn when placed over the baking soda and the vinegar before they were mixed since they do not give off carbon dioxide until they are mixed.

Liquid + Solid = Gas *(cont.)*

Which One Fizzes? Data Sheet

Name _____ Date _____

To the Students: Place a few drops of vinegar on the four powders and write what happens after you test each of them.

Powder	What Happens When Vinegar Is Added?
Flour	
Sugar	
Salt	
Baking Soda	

What Will Rust?

Overview: *Students will experiment with various types of metals to discover those which rust.*

Materials

- assorted small metal items (include steel wool)
- clear plastic cups or baby food jars
- water
- parent letter (page 38)
- Will This Rust? Data Sheet (page 39)
- *optional:* video camera

Lesson Preparation

- Send home the parent letter requesting a variety of metals for this activity.
- Begin this activity on a Monday since the experiment needs at least a week to yield results.

Activity

1. Ask the students if they have ever seen something which has rusted. Tell them that they are going to experiment with a variety of objects to see what will rust and what will not rust.

2. Distribute the parent letter and discuss the types of items students may bring for this experiment.

3. When students have brought their items to school, distribute a data sheet to each of them.

4. Tell the students to put their objects into the cup (jar) and then add just enough water to cover the bottom of the container. If students did not bring steel wool, prepare a jar to test it and assign a student to keep a record of it.

5. Show them how to complete the information on their data sheets, including the day, date, and time for their first drawing. Be sure they are recording as many details as possible.

6. Have students add to their records daily. You may want to make a video record of the changes daily so students can discuss the changes that occurred after the experiment is over.

Closure

- After at least five days, have the students sort the items into two groups, those which rusted and those which did not. List this information on the board. If a video record was made of the items, show it to the class. Ask students to see if they can find anything which those that rusted have in common. (*They should discover that these are all metal but that not all items rusted.*)

- Have students test the items that rusted with a magnet to see if it will pick them up. (*They will be attracted to a magnet since the metals that rusted have iron in them.*)

- After the students test the metals that rusted with their magnets, tell them the metal is iron.

- Tell students to look for signs of rusting metal at school and home and have them share their discoveries with the rest of the class.

What Will Rust? *(cont.)*

Parent Letter for Rust Test

Date_____

Dear Parents,

We are learning about the chemical properties of matter and will be doing experiments to discover what type of matter rusts. Your child has been requested to bring in some type of matter to test. These should be small items which will fit into a baby food jar. We plan to put water into the jar with the object and let the item sit for a week to see if it will rust. We will test items made of metal, glass, plastic, cork, and a variety of other materials. Each student will keep a daily record of the changes they see in the items they are testing.

Some suggestions for the items you might send with your child follow:

- aluminum foil
- bottle caps
- coins
- steel nails
- paper clips

- steel wool
- pebbles
- aluminum nails
- marbles
- cork

Students are encouraged to bring something unusual to test.

Thank you for helping make our experiment interesting. You are welcome to join our class to look at the results of our experiment on_____.

Sincerely,

_____

What Will Rust? *(cont.)*

Will This Rust? Data Sheet

Name:_____ Date:_____

I am testing_____to see if it will rust.
Draw a picture of the thing you are testing every day. Color the picture as carefully as possible to show what the object and water look like. Be sure to write the day, date, and time under each drawing.

Day:_____   Day:_____   Day:_____

Date:_____   Date:_____   Date:_____

Time:_____   Time:_____   Time:_____

Day:_____   Day:_____   Day:_____

Date:_____   Date:_____   Date:_____

Time:_____   Time:_____   Time:_____

Tell what happened to the thing you were testing.

_____

_____

_____

Food + Oxygen = Oxidation

Overview: *Students will observe potatoes and apples as they oxidize.*

Materials

- white potatoes
- lemon juice in squeezable container
- Will It Change? Data Sheet (page 41)
- apples
- paper plates

Lesson Preparation

- Prepare two paper plates for each group, one marked "With Lemon Juice" and the other "Without Lemon Juice."
- Just before the activity begins, cut slices of potatoes and apples so each group will receive two samples of each food. Keep the food in a covered container.

Activity (Adjust the level of discussion as needed.)

1. Discuss the results of the activity Will It Rust? in which the students observed various materials immersed in water. Tell them that the iron rusted because of a chemical change when it was exposed to moisture and oxygen in the air.
2. Say that some foods will also have a chemical reaction that changes them when cut open so oxygen from the air comes in contact with them. Explain that students are going to watch what happens to some food and make a record of the changes they see.
3. Divide students into small groups and give each two paper plates with a slice of potato and apple on each. Add a few drops of lemon juice to each slice on the plate marked "With Lemon Juice."
4. Distribute the data sheet and discuss it with the students to be sure they know what to do.

   To the Teacher: This activity requires that drawings be made of the food when first exposed to air and again two and four hours later. A last drawing is made the next day. Set a timer for the recording intervals to remind students to observe food samples and record results.

Closure

- Have each group share the results of their observations. (*The apple and potato should have turned brown. Slices with lemon juice on them should show less discoloration.*)
- Explain that the lemon juice adds another chemical to the potato and apple that prevents the oxygen from reacting with the chemicals in the food.

Extender

- Have the students test other types of fruits and vegetables (e.g., radish, pear).

Food + Oxygen = Oxidation *(cont.)*

Will It Change? Data Sheet

Name: _____ Date: _____

To the Student: You are going to test apple and potato slices to observe what happens when they are left in the open air. Be sure that you make the drawings of your observations with lots of details to show what you see happening.

Item	What It Looks Like			
	Beginning	After 2 Hours	After 4 Hours	The Next Day
Apple				
Apple with Lemon				
Potato				
Potato with Lemon				

Chemical Magic

Overview: *Students will use red cabbage juice as an indicator dye to identify acids and bases.* (**Note:** This lesson may be spread over two days.)

Materials

- safety goggles for students (See page 48, Delta Education)
- 1/4 head red cabbage
- 1 oz. clear plastic cups (available at stores which supply restaurants)
- dropper bottles or droppers (dropper bottles are available at Delta Education)
- white vinegar
- pure ammonia (without soap)
- Chemical Magic Data Charts (page 44)
- 6 oz. (178 mL) cups for cabbage indicator dye (one per group)
- vials of pH paper with color code (one per group). (See Carolina Biological in Resource section.)
- 3 small glass test tubes and rack

Lesson Preparation

Follow the recipe below to make about a pint of cabbage indicator dye.

Red Cabbage Indicator Dye

Materials: $1/4$ head red cabbage chopped into small pieces water, glass bowl, microwave

Directions: Chop the cabbage into small pieces and place them in the bowl. Add just enough water to cover the cabbage and bring it to a boil. Boil for 3–4 minutes more. Pour the contents into a strainer and drain off the liquid into a container. Refrigerate until ready to use.

Label the 6 oz. (178 mL) cups "cabbage indicator dye" and fill them about $1/2$ full. Place a dropper in each of these cups.

Pour the vinegar and ammonia into dropper bottles and label them. Give each group a set.

(Note: *Ammonia can not be in an open container, due to the fumes. If droppers are used, fill the droppers $1/4$ full, and give one to each group.*)

Fill the test tubes $1/2$ full with the dye and set them in the rack. **Optional:** Use inverted paper or Styrofoam cups with a hole in the bottom just large enough to hold the test tube.

Activity

1. Begin this lesson with a "Magic Show". Place the test tubes with the dye in them where all students can see them. Have ready a vial of pH paper with the color code, and a bottle of ammonia and vinegar with the label concealed. Tell the students you are going to perform a magic show that they are to watch and be ready to write an explanation of what they saw. Follow the steps below.
   - Show the students the test tubes with the blue dye in it and have them note the color.
   - Into one of the tubes place three drops of vinegar and shake it. Let the students observe the color changed from blue to pink (or red).
   - Drop three drops of ammonia into another tube and shake it. Have the students observe that the color of the blue dye is now green.

Chemical Magic *(cont.)*

Activity *(cont.)*

2. Have each student write and draw what they think caused the color change. When they finish this, discuss it with them.

3. Introduce the students to the pH paper and show them the color code inside the bottle. Explain that this is a special paper which changes color to show if something is an acid or base.

   - Take one of the pH strips and place the lower half into the dye with no additives in it. Show the students the color change and hold the paper against the color code to match it. Write the pH number on the board and show that it identifies this as a neutral substance. Repeat this with the other test tubes, showing the dye with vinegar is acid and the ammonia a base.

4. Provide each group with a cup of the dye, three 1 oz. (30 mL) cups, ammonia and vinegar bottles, and a copy of the data chart (page 43). Have them use the dropper to fill the small cups just enough to cover the bottom of it. Tell the students to follow the #1 chart and conduct the tests on the substances. Explain that they should only use one or two drops of the vinegar and ammonia and then, record the results on the chart as they work.

5. Review the results the groups have recorded.

Closure

- Repeat the same tests, but this time provide students with a mystery liquid to test. This should be either an acid or base made by adding a few drops of vinegar or ammonia to 1 oz. (30 mL) cup of water. Do not provide the same mystery liquids to all groups so some will find it a base while others find it an acid.

- Students should use a dropper (or half of a straw) to transfer a few drops of the mystery liquid into the dye. They may use the pH paper dipped into the mystery liquid to get its value.

- After they have identified the mystery liquid as acid or base, reissue the dropper bottles of vinegar and ammonia to them. Have them add drops of the opposite type of liquid to their mystery liquid and test it again.

- Let them repeat this test again, but this time they use the dropper bottle with the matching acid or base as the mystery liquid was originally. **Note:** The groups should use the same container of mystery liquid throughout these tests.

- Discuss their results, all will not be the same. Let them see that as they add the opposite (base or acid) to their mystery liquid, it begins to approach neutral.

Extenders

- Let the students continue adding drops to the mystery liquid to achieve neutral if they can. Their pH paper will be the best identifier for this test.

- Send home the recipe for cabbage indicator dye along with a note to explain what the class has been doing. Encourage the parents to make the dye with their children and repeat the tests, using household items such as tea, shampoo, crushed and liquefied Tums™. Provide a time for the students to report their results to the class.

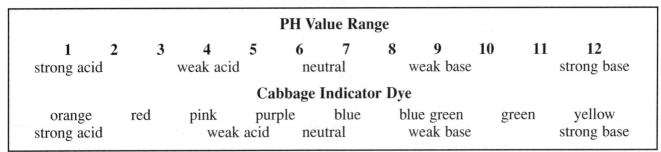

PH Value Range											
1	**2**	**3**	**4**	**5**	**6**	**7**	**8**	**9**	**10**	**11**	**12**
strong acid			weak acid			neutral		weak base			strong base
Cabbage Indicator Dye											
orange		red	pink		purple	blue		blue green		green	yellow
strong acid				weak acid		neutral		weak base			strong base

Chemical Magic *(cont.)*

Chemical Magic Data Charts

To the Teacher: Make copies of these data sheets for each group to have one set.

Group Members			
1. Substances	**Cabbage Dye**	**pH Value**	**Identify liquid** (Circle your answer below.)
water	color:	pH	acid neutral base
vinegar	color:	pH	acid neutral base
ammonia	color:	pH	acid neutral base
2. Substances	**Cabbage Dye**	**pH Value**	**Identify liquid**
mystery liquid	color:	pH	acid neutral base
	color:	pH	acid neutral base
	color:	pH	acid neutral base

Group Members			
1. Substances	**Cabbage Dye**	**pH Value**	**Identify liquid** (Circle your answer below.)
water	color:	pH	acid neutral base
vinegar	color:	pH	acid neutral base
ammonia	color:	pH	acid neutral base
2. Substances	**Cabbage Dye**	**pH Value**	**Identify liquid**
mystery liquid	color:	pH	acid neutral base
	color:	pH	acid neutral base
	color:	pH	acid neutral base

Tasty Chemical Changes

Overview: *Students will combine a variety of matter to make pancakes.*

Materials

- ingredients for pancakes (see recipe)
- electric skillet or griddle for pancakes
- mixing bowl
- paper plates
- cotton swabs
- magnifier for each student
- Tasty Chemical Changes Data Chart (page 47)

- cooking oil or spray
- measuring cups and spoons
- wire whip or electric beater
- plastic forks
- 1-ounce (30 mL) cups
- *optional:* syrup for pancakes

Lesson Preparation

- Set up cooking stations under the supervision of adults or older students. Each of these should have a skillet or griddle, spatula, cooking oil or spray, and paper plates for serving.
- Put tiny samples of the solid ingredients (sour cream, flour, baking soda, salt, cottage cheese) on paper plates for each student.
- Mix up an egg and divide it among the small cups.
- Make a large copy of the recipe to display during this lesson.

Sour Cream Cottage Cheese Pancakes

Ingredients

$^3/_4$ cup (180 mL) sour cream
2 eggs
$^1/_2$ cup (120 mL) cottage cheese

$^1/_2$ cup (120 mL) flour
$^1/_2$ teaspoon (2.5 mL) baking powder
$^1/_2$ teaspoon (2.5 mL) salt

Instructions

- Put sour cream and eggs into the bowl and mix until creamy.
- Add cottage cheese and continue to mix.
- Mix in flour, baking powder, and salt until batter is smooth.
- Let batter stand for 10 minutes. (The chemical reaction between the sour cream and baking soda will create air bubbles and make the pancakes light and fluffy.)
- Bake on lightly greased griddle or skillet.
- Yield: 12 4" (10 cm) pancakes. Increase recipe as needed.

Tasty Chemical Changes *(cont.)*

Activity

To the Teacher: Students may need to work in small groups with an adult or older student to record the information about the matter on their data sheets. This activity can be divided into two sessions—one day for completing the data sheet and the second for making the food.

1. Explain to the students that they are going to help mix different types of matter together to make a chemical change and create something to eat. Tell them that they are going to follow a recipe to make pancakes.

2. Have the students wash their hands, stressing it is important to have clean hands when preparing or eating food.

3. Give each student a data sheet, magnifier, and a plate with samples of the solid ingredients. Distribute the samples of the solids. Tell them to wet one finger and press it into the salt. Have them examine it with a magnifier and record what it looks like. They should rub it between their fingers to feel it. They should also smell and taste each of the samples.

4. Help them describe the salt on their data sheet.

5. Let the students continue this with each of the other solid ingredients. They can taste one of the curds of the cottage cheese. Discuss how to classify the cottage cheese as a solid, a liquid, or both.

6. Distribute cups of the egg. Let them conduct all the tests on the egg, *with the exception of tasting it.*

7. Select volunteers to take turns serving as helpers to make the batter as you mix it. Let them help measure the ingredients into the large bowl and mix it. Increase the recipe to accommodate the number of students.

8. Ask them what happened when they mixed vinegar and baking soda in the Liquid + Solid = Gas activity. (*Bubbles were formed.*) Explain that the batter needs to sit for 10 minutes while the same chemical reaction is taking place between the baking soda and sour cream. Ask them what they think the bubbles will do to the pancakes. (*They make them lighter like a sponge.*)

9. Distribute the batter into a bowl for each cooking station. Assign the students to the various stations to assist and observe the baking process.

Closure

- Let students eat their "science experiment." Have them complete their data sheets.

- Send the recipe home with students so their families may enjoy it.

Tasty Chemical Changes *(cont.)*

Tasty Chemical Changes Data Chart

Name:_____ Date: _____

To the Student: Fill in the chart below to give information about the matter which will be used to make the pancakes.

Matter (Ingredients)	How It Looks, Feels, Smells, and Tastes	State of Matter (solid, liquid, or gas)
salt		
flour		
baking soda		
sour cream		
cottage cheese		
eggs (Do not taste)		

Tell about the way the pancakes look, feel, smell, and taste after they are cooked.

_____

_____

_____

Draw a picture of what the pancake looked like after it was cooked.

Teacher and Student Resources

Related Books

Barber, Jacquelin. *Chemical Reactions.* Order from NSTA or GEMS. (See Below.)

An ordinary resealable plastic bag becomes a safe and spectacular laboratory as students mix chemicals that bubble, change color, get hot, and produce gas, heat, and odor. This exciting unit explores chemical change, demonstrates endothermic and exothermic reactions, and develops skills in observation, experimentation, and inference.

Bosak, Susan. *Science Is...A Sourcebook of Fascinating, Fact, Projects, and Activities.* Scholastic Canada, LTC. (1992) This book is packed full of hands-on experiments covering a wide range of science topics, including matter. This book may be ordered from NSTA. (See below.)

O'Brien-Palmer, Michelle. *Sense-Abilities: Fun Ways to Explore the Senses.* (1998) Students explore the five senses, funny songs, 74 activities to inspire children to discover.
Order from NSTA. (See Below.)

Sarquis, M. & Williams, J. *Teaching Chemistry with Toys.*

Innovative activities using everyday toys to demonstrate the principles of chemistry is ways children in grades K - 9 can easily understand. Order from NSTA. (See Below.)

Suppliers of Science Materials

Carolina Biological (800) 334-5551 **http://www.carolina.com/**

Hydrion Jumbo pH Strips, Wide Range 5 vials with color code WW-89-5280 $15. (15 per package)

Delta Education (800) 282-9560. Request a catalog of materials or order online at their Website.
http://www.delta-education.com/corp/info/ordernow.html

Supplies a wide variety of materials to support hands-on science in all areas from elementary to middle school. This includes dropper bottles.

National Science Resource Center http://www.si.edu/nsrc/

Resources for Teaching Elementary Science. National Science Resource Center, National Academy Press, Washington, DC. 1996. This outstanding resource guide to hands-on inquiry-centered elementary science curriculum materials and resources. Each reference in this guide has been carefully evaluated and is fully described, including addresses.

Read this book online or order it from: **http://www.nap.edu/catalog/4966.html**

National Science Teachers Association (NSTA)

http://www.nsta.org/ or the online catalog of materials at **http://store.nsta.org/**

This outstanding organization, founded in 1944, has a membership of 53,000, which includes science teachers, science supervisors, administrators, scientists, and business and industry. Members receive a monthly journal, the bimonthly NSTA Reports, discounts at the regional and national conventions, and an annual catalog of materials.

Great Explorations in Math and Science (GEMS)
http://www.lhs.berkeley.edu/GEMS/gemsguides.html

Directly from the Lawrence Hall of Science at UC Berkeley comes great teacher guides in a wide range of science topics. Check out their Website to see all that is available.